Lord, Let's Talk Again Today

Phyllis W. Gray

ISBN-10:1479189251
ISBN-13:9781479189250

DEDICATION

This book is dedicated to all those who read the first book and encouraged me to continue writing. Your words of encouragement have meant so much to me and I write in hopes that many others will be blessed by this book. Most of all I dedicate it to my Lord, who is the real author and grateful to Him for all the inspiration He has given me through these words. I would like to thank my husband, Ike for all his help and proofing that helped get this to the publishing stage. His encouragement has meant so very much to me and his belief in me that I could write once again.

CONTENTS

Introduction

I would have never believed that people living in America, who attend church on a regular basis would be so word starved.

I am so thankful for my upbringing and instilled knowledge of God and His Word.

Looking back over the years and the things that have transpired in my life, I could have never come this far without depending upon His Word and the direction it has given me.

God's Word gives us faith, hope, and direction when the world gives us none.

Many times, my situation would have been totally hopeless without knowing what God's Word said about it.

I have learned to seek God's Word first when I have a problem. If I try to solve it on my own, not only do I waste time, but sometimes I make it worse than it was.

God's Word has an answer to every problem you will ever encounter. Oh, it may not be what you always expect or want to hear, but the answer is there.

Every subject is covered, yet if it's not what the world or the evening news says, people tend to say that it isn't for today!

Well, the Word doesn't change. It never has. People change. The expectations and desires of man change but not God or His Word. Hebrews 13:8, "Jesus Christ is the same, yesterday, today and forever". That means nothing from the beginning has ever changed because in the beginning was the Word and the Word became flesh and dwelt among us. That is what the book of John says and I believe it. I am stunned at how people accept the morals in today's society. Without a word based life, people are easily influenced by the outside media sources that promote all kinds of immoral activity.

The scripture says without faith it is impossible to please God, so that said, there are millions of people who love the Lord, but aren't pleasing Him.

How can we change? By spending time with the Lord, not just a simple prayer at meal time, but quality, quiet time even if it's fifteen minutes in the morning before you start your day.

How can we start a day that is productive without His direction?

My prayer is that you will glean a hunger for God's Word and the messages that follow in this book will inspire you, build your faith and help you build a greater desire to search the scriptures for every answer you need in days ahead. Never forget, He has every answer you will ever need...He loves you so much!

Oh Lord, You have heard the desire and the longing of the humble and oppressed. You will prepare and strengthen and direct their hearts; you will cause your ear to hear.
Psalm 10:17

Chapter 1

Lord, Prepare My Heart

Only God can look into the heart of man. He sees all the desires, the good, the bad and the ugly, so to speak.

The scripture says He will prepare and strengthen our hearts, but we have to be willing and submissive to His will. Psalm 26:2 says, "Examine me, O Lord and prove me; test my heart and my mind".

When we pray, read the word and get in the presence of the Lord, He is able to show us what we need to change. He will get into the depths of our heart and pull out things we've hidden away and let us see how they really are. Then He allows us to deal with them.

The Lord will never force us to change or let go of the things we should, but He will show us what we need to do and leave the decision to us.

If we aren't willing to make changes in our lives, we will never grow spiritually beyond where we are. We will stay chained to the past and never know where we could have gone with the Lord.

God already knows the hidden secrets of our heart. He knows well before He reminds us. He sees every thought and motive of our very being and desires us to let go of the things that do not line up with His Word.

God is not blind to our hidden secrets and sins. We hide nothing from Him. If our heart is truly after the Lord, then we want everything that is hidden exposed so we can deal with it. Light always exposes darkness and when we are in His presence, light is present and sin is exposed.

The more light we walk in, the more truth we will live in. Quickly, we will react to anything contrary to God and His Word. Deception cannot take hold of our lives when we walk in the light. The Holy Spirit will expose it and reveal it to us every time.

Listen to the spirit of God in your life. Allow Him to examine your heart and reveal anything you need to release or change.

We all want to grow in our faith and draw closer to the Lord. We must be willing to do a heart exam and allow the Lord to expose anything we need to fix.

We must do self-examinations on a continual basis and stay in the Word. The Word will wash us and clean us from all unrighteousness. It will bring to our mind, anything we need to seek the Lord about. The Word like God's love, will never condemn us but convict us of our sins so we can repent and move on in His love and grow in His wisdom.

Lord, you are so good to remind me that you know all about me and my motives of heart. Help me to clean up anything not pleasing to you and feel free to show me any area of my life that I need to change so I can become more like you........................

BELOVED LET US LOVE ONE
ANOTHER, FOR LOVE IS OF GOD;
AND EVERYONE WHO LOVES IS
BORN OF GOD AND KNOWS GOD.
I JOHN 4:7

Chapter 2

When Life and Love Hurt

Loving and living your life with joy isn't always easy. Every day there are obstacles in our path to change our direction or way of living. Just because we decide to walk in love with others, doesn't mean they will return it to us.

When love isn't returned and comes back to us as disfavor or rejection, it hurts. Does it mean we should stop walking in that love with those who refuse to return it? The answer is an emphatic no! That is all the more reason to give love again and again. When your love toward others is rejected, it is not at you but God. Brotherly love is a commandment.

God's Word says we are to love one another as He loves us. His love is unconditional, not because we earn it or deserve it, but because He is love.

We are called to that same walk. There may be those who don't like you and simply, you make them uncomfortable because the love of God is in you, yet, you must continue to love them as God loves you, in spite of how bad their actions hurt or the rejection you feel.

Love always wins! It can never be discarded without a consequence. You may not see the results, but the love you give to another person will bring a change in their life. It will cause them to make a choice concerning the love given to them from the actions of another. They decide how they will receive or reject the love and either way it will have a lasting impact on their life.

Some people hurt so much they have a difficult time receiving love from anyone. As love continues over and over to reach out, without ceasing, it will eventually begin to penetrate the shell of hurt and melt the shield of their heart.

You cannot be saturated in love and not get wet.

Allow God's love to heal any hurts you have. Ask Him to show you how to give love unconditionally that others may see Him in your life.

Begin to see others through God's eyes. He will show you their hearts so you can pray for them and love them because you have an understanding of what they may be feeling.

His love never, never fails and you will have joy unspeakable and full of glory if you just continue the love walk with everyone God places in your path. Your life will be richer, fuller, and so blessed as you allow the Lord to direct your life and actions.

Your hurt won't seem so significant if you are trying to bless others who are hurting. In fact, as you give love it will be given back many times over. It may not be from the ones you are giving to, but it will come when you most need it and it will bless you more than you could have possibly imagined.

From the beginning of time, God made every provision for man to walk in love with one another. He left no room for failure.

You are created in His image and if He is in your heart, then you can live and operate in that God kind of love. Allow Him to fill your heart with His love. Then, begin to give it to all around you, regardless of how you are treated. Your capacity for love will expand beyond anything you've ever known and reaching out in love will become as natural as breathing.

God's love is reaching out to you right now, this very minute. Receive all He has to give you. You will become a reservoir of love that will spill on to everyone you meet.

Open your heart and feel His love expanding you and filling you to be a vessel of blessing.

Now go pour it out over and over. Your vessel will never be empty again. The more you pour out, the quicker you will receive more, and then more.

A vessel of God's love is what you are. Go now, and flood some lives with God's love. You will never be able to give out more than you receive. It multiplies when given away.

Do you need to feel loved: then go love someone that needs a hug or a pat on the back. Give someone a call and tell them you love them. Watch God work to begin to send love in so many ways to you. It will come because His Word says so. Get ready to be loved!

Phyllis W. Gray

*I cried out to the Lord because of my
affliction, and He answered me.*
                        Jonah 2:2

Chapter 3

Lord, I Can't Take it Anymore

Have you ever heard anyone say, "I can't take it anymore"? It's a point we have all been to. Some call it flipping out...I'm going nuts or I'm losing it or I'm going crazy!

We have heard, I am fed up, at my wits end or at my breaking point. Does that sound familiar?

Jesus, in Luke 22 had sweat as drops of blood pouring out of His pores. This was pre-calvary. He knew He was going to die and that He would suffer an excruciating death.

He was at the point he didn't know if He could take this and He ask the Father if He would remove the cup of suffering from Him if He was willing, yet He said, "nevertheless, not my will but thy will be done".

If we look further in God's Word, there are three other people whose names begin with "J" who reached the point of , "I can't take it anymore".

Jonah – Jonah chapter 1 says this. Now the word of the Lord came unto Jonah, the son of Amittai saying, "Arise, go to Nineveh, the great city, and cry against it for their wickedness has come up before me".

What is difficult to understand about those words? The word of the Lord came to him and said, "Arise" That means get up, go to Nineveh. This is like God saying, "go to Wal-Mart".

15

He didn't say go to K-Mart or to Roses. He said Wal-Mart.

Jonah got a word from God, a clear word. He disobeyed.
When you disobey God's Word, you are setting yourself up.
Verse three says, but Jonah. Those are terrible words in the
Bible! But Jonah rose up to flee to Tarshish from the
presence of the Lord. He went the opposite way.
He gets on a boat with a bunch of merchant marines and
they have a cargo to deliver, but because there is a man of
God disobeying God, he brings everyone on the ship into
jeopardy. After casting lots, they throw Jonah overboard.
This was not God's plan, but at the end of Chapter one we see
that Jonah is swallowed by a fish. Then in Chapter 2: verse 7
he remembers the Lord. He finally came to desperation!

Judas – Judas betrayed Jesus. In Matthew 26:14 it tells how
he accomplished it. Then in Matthew 27, after Jesus was
betrayed, Judas, sees in verse three that he was condemned.
He repented and brought the 30 pieces of silver to the chief
priest and told him that he had sinned by betraying innocent
blood. But it was too late he thought and he came to a crisis
and hanged himself in desperation.

Jailer – In Acts: 16:23, Paul and Silas were whipped,
shackled and thrown in prison. The jailer who was put in
charge, was ordered to watch those two and told he was
responsible for them. Scripture says that Paul and Silas were
praying and praising God and a great earthquake shook the
jail and the doors all opened and the shackles fell off the
prisoners. The jailer knew he was done for and just couldn't
take it anymore. He lifted his sword to kill himself when
Paul told him they were all there. He ask them what he had
to do to be saved and he and his family ended up being
baptized. He was desperate.

"I can't take it anymore" is a place of desperation. It is the
loss of hope and the surrender to circumstances. Jonah
reached desperation. He had gotten a direct word from the
Lord, but because he disobeyed, he lost his hope in sin.

Judas reached a place of desperation. He was a follower of Jesus, but he backslid. A backslider is on fire for God then things don't work the way they think, so they back away. Judas became frustrated because he began to wonder what he was going to get out of following Jesus. He reached desperation.

The jailer was desperate. He was doing fine until the earthquake. Suddenly, he saw the prisoners loose and the jail was falling down, the doors opened. He's in charge and there is no hope. He has lost his job and even his life. It's desperation time for him.

After desperation, there is danger. Danger is irrational thinking. You do things you wouldn't normally do.

Jonah disobeys God, gets in a boat, falls asleep and puts everyone in danger. Judas stepped out from under God's umbrella of protection. As long as he walked with Jesus, he was under His protection. Have you ever done that. Something goes wrong and you quit praying and seeking the Lord. You rely on what you have heard in the past and the rain from Hell begins to fall on you.

Any time you get to where you can't take it and don't call on the Lord, the devil is right there ready to push you over the edge. He wants you to take your life or depend on drugs, alcohol or some other crutch that will harm you.

Then it's time for a decision. Jonah decided in the belly of that fish to do what God has told him. Judas came to the decision that he couldn't live with what he had done. The jailer came to that point and wanted to know what he had to do in order to change his life.

All of us make decisions every day that affects our lives continually. If you get to the end of your rope then you must make a decision.

When you are ready to make a decision, then God is waiting for you. He is ready to forgive you, ready to give you hope again and if you will trust Him and His Word more than the circumstances you are in, He will show you the way to a new day.

If you can't take it anymore, then God is there waiting to take your burdens. He has the answers for all your problems. He has had them all along. He has just been waiting for you to call out to Him and let Him give you everything you need to live a peaceful, productive life.

Remember, when you can't, He can. He is a God of a second chance.....

Take your burdens to Him now.....he's been waiting for you.

No man can serve two masters, for either he will hate the one and love the other; or else he will hold to the one and despise the other. You cannot serve God and mammon. (Matthew 6:24)

Chapter 4

Confusion Breeds Compromise

Today there is such confusion in the Body of Christ. Why? The church has been guilty of trying to serve flesh and spirit. She cannot do both! Therefore by trying to do so she stands at a crossroads and is motionless trying to make a decision as to which way to go. She wants to please God, yet, she likes to please man also.

God's Word plainly states in Matthew 6:24, "No man can serve two masters, for either he will hate the one and love the other; or else he will hold to the one, and despise the other. Ye cannot serve God and mammon."

The Church has taken Her eyes off God and His Word and allowed all the worldly demands to get Her in a state of confusion. Do we go along with man in order to try to win more of Christ or do we stick by the Book and not waiver, allowing the Lord to do the drawing? Who do we listen to anymore? Everyone seems to be talking.

Confusion causes hasty decisions. One of my favorite scriptures is Isaiah 40:31, "But they that wait upon the Lord shall renew their strength; they shall mount up with wings as eagles; they shall run and not be weary; and they shall walk and not faint." This means what it says. When we wait on the Lord for instructions, then we are led by His will and not our own. In the Strong's Concordance, the word, "strength" means to be firm, to produce, to have might, power and wealth.

In Vine's Dictionary, strength means power and authority. Oh, if we could just hear what this is saying and do it every day. God wants to bless us, equip us, prepare us and anoint us to do what He's calling us to do and to go where He 's leading us. We mess up when we get in a hurry and get tired of waiting and doing nothing and then just go and do what we think is right or what someone expects of us.

Man's expectations have steered many in the wrong direction. If they had just waited to get the Lord's direction, they would have prospered and been blessed in the mission the Lord would have given them.

Let us not get hasty by listening to voices other than the Lord. Satan is the author of confusion and he likes to get us so confused that we hear everyone but the Lord.

We'll not grow weary in that place and we'll not burn out or faint in the midst of what we've been called to do. He'll even give us the swiftness of the eagle as if we have supernatural wings. Glory to God, let's learn to wait and not get hasty.

We can be content where we are and rejoice over our past blessings with the Lord. We can be satisfied with what the Lord has done in our lives and how He has given us past revelations that we walked in. Now, we've come to a mountain of decision making or a fork in the path we're on. We must decide if we are going to stay where we are or if we are going to get out of the habit of moving or doing just because it feels good to our flesh. God has not taken us out of Egypt to send us back again. He wants us to grow up in Him and to be able to hear His instructions and be able to follow them, no matter what the cost.

God isn't looking for a few good men. He is looking for a ʾ who will come close to Him and lay down their past nd inhibitions. Exodus 20:18-21 talks about how the ʾtood afar off and would not come near the mountain.

They were afraid of His presence. God wanted all the people to come close, not just Moses. He wanted all the Israelites to see the land of promise.

We cannot shrink back from what God is doing and from His presence today. If we do, we are sealing our future.

We are truly at a crossroads today. One way leads to the presence of the Lord, and the other way leads us back to where we came from in the religious church setting; being fed and then lying down, sleeping and growing fat and lazy.

If we don't make the decision to hear God and follow His instructions, then we are going to be led down the wrong road of compromise. We'll justify anything we are doing as being in the Lord's will and yet there will be absolutely no fruit from our efforts.

A decision to draw close to the Lord requires commitment. There must be a willingness to lay aside the things of the world, the past experiences ,blessings and the religious expectations we've had. We have to decide to go on with the Lord no matter what the price, ask Him to take us to a higher level of commitment and be willing to lay down any plans we 've had and pray. "God, what is it You want me to do, I'm willing".

There is therefore now no condemnation to them which are in Christ Jesus, who walk not after the flesh, but after the Spirit.
(Romans 8:1)

Chapter 5

Commitment – Death to the Flesh

When we are totally committed to something it means we cannot allow any outside influence to stop us from staying on course or staying dedicated to that purpose.

The devil fights really hard when he knows we are sold out to Jesus and are seeking Him and His presence with our all. He will send every diversion he possibly can to cause us to lose sight of what we are seeking. We have to not be moved by what we see nor what we hear from anyone other than the Spirit of God. Our spiritual ears and spiritual eyes should be the only ones leading us by His spirit. We can't listen to man or be influenced by what we see others do. God may have called you to a different task and you can't do what you're to do if you keep your eyes on another person rather than the Lord.

Commitment is singleness of purpose and of sight. If we keep our eyes on Jesus, then we won't see the smoke screens the enemy sends or hear the gossipers that try to stir up strife in our midst. When we keep our spiritual ears in tune with the Holy Spirit Network, then the things of this world just become so faint that we hardly notice them.

The world tries to make us think as Christians, we are crazy or out on the deep end because of our convictions. This causes many who are led by the flesh to compromise and let down their guard somewhat in order to be a part of the accepted crowd.

Romans 8:1 says, "There is therefore now no condemnation to them which are in Christ Jesus, who walk not after the flesh, but after the Spirit". If we are being led by God's Spirit, it won't matter what anyone else thinks. We are dead to that emotional realm of feeling set apart, and our relationship with Christ is the foremost thing on our mind continually and pleasing Him takes first place in our life.

Verse 6 of that same passage says that to be spiritually minded is life and peace. When we try to do something in the natural that doesn't agree with the Spirit of God in us, we are not at peace. On the contrary, we are confused, troubled, and many times feel separated from God's presence. Then the enemy likes to send strife and confusion so that we will be ill at ease with everything and everyone and that causes total unrest in our lives.

Our problem many times is that we cannot get still long enough to hear what the Spirit of God is speaking to us and we think surely He is moving in our lives this way or that way because that is how He is moving in Brother So-in-so's life. We have all been guilty of trying to hurry God in to speaking a quick word to us. He is not a hurrying God, but He's an on time God. He always moves at the right time and in the right way for our particular circumstances if we are praying, trusting and releasing our will to His.

Our God always wants to give us His best in all situations, but we hinder that move many times by our inability to wait on Him. We are not walking by His Spirit, because we need an answer now and spoil the move of God that would have blessed us abundantly.

If we walk continually by His Spirit, we will learn to not get in a hurry, but to wait patiently upon His move in the situation, knowing He will give us the answer that is in our best interest and that is according to His will, not ours, and that will bring peace and abundant blessing to us.

We have no need to get upset and look to the left and then to the right for our answers. We simply need to rest in those promises and learn to come to an end of all self-motivated activity and become comfortable with divine activity.

We so need to learn how to cease from working for the Lord in His absence, to responding to and cooperating with the Lord in His presence.

The Lord wants to visit His people so much and He wants to see if we can rest in Him and make room in our busy schedule and our organized and timed church services.

We have been so active that we become impatient with inactivity and are unable to rest.

With our busyness, all of our efforts have not accomplished the purpose of the Lord to establish righteousness, peace and joy upon the earth. Therefore, we must come to a cessation of "our methods" in order to make room for the Lord to become active to accomplish that which we were unable to do.

God wants us to enter into His rest that we may enter into His presence and then He can come with His visitations full of power and glory.

Phyllis W. Gray

They that wait upon the Lord shall renew their strength; they shall mount up with wings as eagles; they shall run and not be weary; they shall walk and not faint....(Isaiah 40:31)

Chapter 6

Waiting Upon the Lord

Our lives in today's fast pace is often times drained of strength and then we grow weary and are of little use to ourselves or God. We are a society of hurry and run people and never slow down to allow the Lord to speak to us or direct us in the way He would have us go. We think and plan in temporal terms while God is interested in eternity.

Hurrying and being out of God's will robs our strength. Neh. 8:10 says, "the joy of the Lord is our strength". The eagle spends a lot of time waiting in life and it's in the waiting that his strength is renewed and he can ride the winds and soar above every storm and see farther than all other birds. He is strong and mighty because he has learned to wait. It's a matter of life or death to him. It can be to us as well!

It is more critical than ever now in the times we are living in to make sure we're hearing the Lord. Sometimes we get so anxious to serve the Lord we take off on a tangent and we are working like mad in the flesh and there's no Spirit of God to be found in it.

It's not always easy to "wait" when we get an idea we think would bless God. Then when things don't work out the way we imagined, we just can't understand and blame the devil for messing up "God's" plan when He wasn't even a part of it.

Praying about a desire or idea seems like such a waste of time when we could be out there getting things done. Without prayer, and direction from the Lord, these works are simply wood, hay, and stubble.

Learning to wait upon Him teaches us patience which is lacking greatly today in the Body of Christ.

We should not be found in the position where the Lord has to "look for us" in our busy schedule. It is very important that we set apart that time to be in His presence and then respond to His desire for our fellowship. The Lord wants to prepare us for what is about to take place in this end-time hour. We must have ears to hear what the Spirit is saying and then heed what is said.

We are in a time of transition in the Body of Christ. For so long we have hum drummed along as if we have a lifetime to get done what needs to be done now. We have become so accustomed to doing it our way and on our schedule that we have difficulty shifting from working for the Lord in His absence, to responding and cooperating with the Lord in His presence. This means we must come to the end of a self-motivated activity and enter a "state of rest".

The problem is that we've been so active that we become impatient with inactivity and are unable to rest.

We must come to an end of "our methods" in order to make room for the Lord to become active to accomplish that which we are unable to do.

God can only move when we are willing to get out of the way. When we "let go and let God", then we see mighty things begin to happen.

It is a very hard thing in the natural for us to sit back and rest when we see something that needs to be done, but this is how we become so busy that we can't hear the Lord speak or see Him in our everyday activities when He moves. We pray about a situation and before we give the Lord a chance to answer, we get busy trying to fix it ourselves.

Why can't we begin to pray, and wait on the Lord and enter into His rest until we hear from Him or our request is answered? We serve a big God and He is able to do what needs to be done in our lives and the lives of others by using us or by having us on our knees interceding for someone else to do the work. Whatever the assignment, the Lord has for us, it cannot be accomplished unless we rest in the Lord and hear from Him.

As we wait on the Lord and rest in His presence, He is able to speak to us and allow us to look within as He unveils our heart. Then the cleansing process begins and those hidden places are revealed that we may release the hurts and be made whole in every area.

Malachi 3:6 says, "the Lord whom you seek will suddenly come to His temple". As we restore the dwelling place within us to purity and cleanse our hearts for Him, the Lord will come "suddenly" in our midst.

Cleansing must become a way of life but it doesn't have to take a lifetime. It is in the time when we release the cares of the world and sit at His feet by entering into His presence that this deep cleansing and restoration happens. We all need a time of cleansing often.

The Lord desires to do a total work within each of our lives. He desires that our entire lives become a testimony of Him, not just through our words, but through our lives.

In His goodness, He is stirring us in regards to our loving one another, for without love, we are but sounding brass. The Lord is not causing "sounding brass" to come forth, rather He is creating trumpets, voices in this day who will speak the pure word of the Lord.

Before the fall, the Lord walked with Adam in the cool of the evening. When Adam fell, he broke that relationship and hid from the presence of the Lord. The very thing that the Lord did was to look for Adam. He called out to Adam and said, "Where are You?" The Lord certainly knew where Adam was, but intensely desired the place of fellowship that He once had with him.

We should not be found in the position where the Lord has to "look for us" in our busy schedule. It is extremely important that we set apart time to be in His presence and then respond to His desire for our fellowship. As we become quiet enough to listen, He will be heard saying to us, "Where are you?" The Lord wants us to learn to wait on Him by having ears to hear and heed what is said by the Spirit of God.

Wait on the Lord, and you will find renewed strength for your life and all your days ahead.

For this reason I am telling you, whatever you ask for in prayer, believe, trust and be confident, that it is granted to you, and you will get it. (Amplified Bible Mark 11:24)

Chapter 7

In God's Eyes – Delays Are Not Denials

We pray as diligent as we can and believe for results. Nothing happens. We continue to pray and believe and still the prayer isn't answered.

We then feel God must not have heard our prayer, or He just didn't want to answer it. That thinking is far from the truth. If we are in fellowship with the Lord and trusting His Word for our direction, then He hears our prayers.

We are not always on the same timetable as He is. If every prayer we prayed was answered immediately, we may find ourselves in a great deal of trouble, and nevertheless, where would our faith level be.

When we believe for something, not seeing any evidence of it, until it comes to pass; that is faith. Faith, the substance of things hoped for, the evidence of things not seen.

All we have to stand on is His Word, our prayers and faith to believe what we have prayed will come to pass. We can't plant tomato seeds and look for tomatoes the next day or week. It takes time for the seed to produce a plant and then a crop.

When we pray God's Word over a situation or something we desire, it's like planting a seed. After we plant the seed in prayer we can dig it back up with our negative words. That is called being double minded.

We can't pray for it and then confess that it's just not going to happen.

We must continue to agree with God's Word concerning what we are believing for, thanking Him for the answer and manifestation of our prayer until we see the results.

After we have prayed we must lay the request at the feet of Jesus, stand on the Word and wait expectantly for the answer.

God is an on time God. He's never too early and He's never too late but He is there at the right time.

God knows ahead what the end result will be. He knows if the prayer we prayed will result in peace or turmoil, and He knows if the prayer was in line with His Word and His will for our lives.

When we pray, our words must line up with God's Word and His will. We must pray daily to know what His will for our life is and He will make it plain to us.

He will never answer prayers contrary to His Word. We cannot pray bad things against another person and expect Him to answer, nor for things that bring evil.

When we pray for others, their will is also involved and God will never force a person to make changes in their life.

We may pray for someone for years before we see results. All along the Lord was moving in that person's life, but they had to choose to change before the prayers could be answered.

We must learn to never give up when we pray for something if it is in line with God's Word. Get pregnant with expectancy for the results. Everyday speak of the results and thank God for it. The Word says Jesus spoke of things that were not, as though they were. We have to believe so strongly that God will grant the answer we've prayed for, that we act like and confess the answer until we see it come to pass.

Just because we can't see the answer to our prayers right away, never means God won't answer or He didn't hear us.

Keep praying, believing, confessing, expecting and then wait until the answer comes. Give it time. Allow your faith to grow and you will see results.

Phyllis W. Gray

Then they cry out to the Lord in their trouble, and He brings them out of their distresses. He calms the storm so that the waves are still.
(Psalm 107:28-29)

Phyllis W. Gray

Chapter 8

Storm Clouds on the Horizon—Warning Approaching Storms!

How many times have we heard predictions of approaching storms and laughed it off to later see that we should have listened and took shelter?

The sun is shining, the sky is blue and nothing gives the indication of an approaching storm, but we have been warned and yet, because we can't see anything to indicate bad weather, we ignore it.

This same thing happens in the storms of life. We are too busy to look and listen and hear the Spirit of God.

In our natural, everyday lives we often fail to take the time to listen and then we wonder how we could have been caught off guard when the storms of life come upon us. We need to keep our spirit man stronger than the flesh at all times, by the Word of God, praying, fasting and staying in in the presence of God.

Today, there is a big thing about working out at the gym, building muscle, burning fat and staying fit. I couldn't agree more, but do we spend as much time in the Word, building our spirit man . Our flesh is fed by worldly things and our spirit is fed from the Spirit of God.

Many times people may think us strange when we're

preparing our spirit man for things to come. Then, as we prepare our spirit, the Lord shows us other things we need to take care of in the natural.

We can't even imagine what it must have been like when God told Noah to build an Ark. (Gen. 6:6). It had never rained and this man was preparing for a flood. He was surely the nut of all nuts, but when the storm finally came, he and his family floated and everyone else sank.

I am sure he spent many hours and days hearing the Lord and following His instructions. He could have easily quit and have been swayed by the crowd, but he chose to put his trust and faith in his God rather than man. He prepared while the sun was shining and there wasn't a cloud in the sky. If he had waited until God showed him rain clouds, it would have been too late.

Sometimes we like to wait on visible signs and confirmations from half a dozen sources and will even doubt that we heard God unless everyone agrees. Then instead of obeying the Spirit of God, we will wait until we're caught off guard and unprepared for what comes and then we blame God for not warning us.

How can we see and still not believe? The Lord is telling us today to stop –look –listen! Stop the business, stop the procrastination, stop being led by the crowd, and stop the influence of all other worldly pulls.

Listening is something many of us have trouble with. It's easy to talk but hard to listen, especially to the Spirit of God. Why? A lot of the time the Spirit doesn't want to agree with the flesh and the flesh wins out when we don't have time to just sit and listen.

Listen means to hear and heed what you've heard. We may hear but don't do what we know we should.

We make excuses or compromise what we have heard to satisfy that old flesh nature so everything will be comfortable and no one will get upset.

Our flesh had rather be accepted by man than to be obedient to God.

Disobedience is rebellion and rebellion is witchcraft. It's time we begin to take a stand to be obedient to God, no matter how much it displeases man. If man's heart is after the Lord, he won't be in displeasure.

When storms come, change comes. Many times change comes by destruction, and much of this is because man wasn't prepared and didn't heed warnings. Then we stand and say, "Why Lord", instead of "Yes Lord". "Why change Lord, I liked things the way they were? Yes Lord, I don't understand, but show me what I need to change in my life. Lord, show me how to prepare myself to be in obedience to you and your Word".

With "why" comes all kinds of excuses. We could come up with hundreds of reasons why things should have not happened.

With "yes" comes acknowledgement of the situation and a desire to allow the Lord to bring change into your life in order to make you grow.

Storms will always come, but how we handle them and the consequences then depends on what we do before they come. Some would say, "I'm not preparing for something I don't want to come. That's like asking it to come". No, the Lord tells us in His Word that there will be tribulation , but we have overcome, only if we prepare to be overcomers.

An overcomer is one who sees or senses what is coming and makes himself ready for it and goes over whatever comes.

An overcomer is not someone who folds his hands and sits back and refuses to believe anything offensive will ever come his way. He's living in a dream world.

All through the scriptures, God always told the people how to prepare for storms that came. Those who followed His instructions overcame. Those who didn't were overcome.

The people who continually ask God, "Why", are most times the ones who are never willing to spend quiet time with Him to get their answers. God wants to tell us "Why", He wants changes in our lives, but we don't want to really hear because it makes us responsible for what we've heard.

The chronic "whyers" are usually the "whiners", who just want man to feel sorry for them because bad things always happen to them.

A magnet draws things to itself. You need to get alone with the Lord and get demagnetized from the world and you won't continually draw bad things from the world, but then good things by the Spirit of God will begin to come your way.

You will then hear or sense warnings by the Spirit of God. He'll show you weak places in your walk before you become vulnerable for the enemy to strike. When you live by the Spirit of God, you live in a state of preparedness, always ready when storms come. You will not be caught off guard.

We can't wait until bad things happen and then start preparing. We must make ourselves ready daily, and learn to listen to His voice.

Listen to what He is saying in your life. Hear His plan. He will tell you what you need to change spiritually and physically.

We are of no use to God or anyone if we allow the enemy to destroy our body. When we are so busy with things and doing fleshly tasks, we become blind to what the Spirit is saying and we allow storms to come and cause our body to shipwreck.

Just as God told Noah to build an ark, He wants to prepare us spiritually and physically to stand strong against any storm that comes and we will overcome because we have heard and heeded what the Lord has said.

Storms will come. How will you handle them? Only you can answer that. Let the Lord prepare you now for what may be on the horizon.

Then I will give them a heart to know me, that I am the Lord; and they shall be My people, and I will be their God, for they shall return to Me with their whole heart.
(Jeremiah 24:7)

Chapter 9

What's Your Sign?

What does your sign read? We all wear a sign whether we are aware of it or not. Churches, also wear signs and nations wear signs. The important thing is, what does your sign say?

If you know, then you might be able to understand why things are happening the way they are in your life.

Are you blessed and at total peace? Despite opposition, is everything flowing smoothly? Okay, you sense a powerful anointing from God in every area of your life. Protection and health are yours and your family's. No weapons are forming against you.

Then again, every time you move out to do what you believe God is saying do, you run up against a wall, over and over. You don't see your dreams being fulfilled. You struggle to see blessings. You're under constant attack and it seems the enemy keep slipping those arrows in. Your finances are being attacked; your health and that of your family is constantly attacked. You just can't seem to flow in the anointing of God and you can't find peace and your whole life seems to be in constant turmoil.

You might be wearing an invisible sign you aren't aware of. Men can't see the sign but the devil certainly sees it, through what you believe and what you are putting into practice in your life.

There are two signs. One reads, "Fully Operational, Powered by the Holy Spirit". The other one reads, "Out of Order, Powered by Man's Will.

The first sign is a signal to the enemy to back off or be defeated. No door is open, no crack unfilled, all attacks will be fruitless.

The next sign lets the enemy know, there are ways in to torment, to harass, to steal joy and peace.

How can this be? You are saying, "I love the Lord and I am walking in the Spirit. I am definitely not out of order". Funny you would say that, because that is a sure sign that something might be wrong. You fail to believe you could possibly be missing God.

Lawlessness and obedience are two sides of the same coin. Man has the choice of which side he will choose. Is it possible to know and understand the things of the spirit and yet, go our own way? YES!

A disobedient spirit is one who sees the need for something to be done and yet, God hasn't said to do it. He goes ahead and does it anyway.

You want to do something for Jesus, your promotions, your plans, your trips, your agenda, but it's not what God said. It's disobedience and it's lawlessness.

No one has trouble obeying until God's will crosses his will.

Psalm 19 has much to teach us along these things. It shows us in verse 3 the ways God makes Himself known to man.
1. General revelation
2. Special revelation
3. Spiritual revelation – where God makes Himself known through the Spirit in the inner man.

Verses 1-6 gives us general revelation. Pictured for us is a man looking upward. He sees the heavens spread before him. He sees the light, the dark, and the stars. One sees it as the glories proclaim the creations of God, and to another just questions with no answers.

There is no voice, no speech, yet, people get excited because they see evidence of His creative powers and even the devils believe in God.

General revelation is a step in the right direction. It tells you who He is but not His will for you.

Verses 7-11 contains a special revelation of God. Special revelation shows us His provisions for all of our needs and in this we get a picture of His greatness, his goodness and his wisdom.

He also tells us what He wants us to do, where He wants us to go, what to say, how to dress, and what He expects from us.

In verse 12-14, we see spiritual revelation. It occurs when God works what He is and what He reveals Himself to be into the heart of man.

Jeremiah, Ezekiel and the Book of Hebrews all teach us that God's ultimate goal is to open us up and write His laws on our hearts.

In Jeremiah the word says.... "I will give him a new heart". In Ezekiel the word states.... "I will sprinkle you and write my laws on your heart". In Hebrews 8 and 10, the scripture says.... "I write my laws on your heart".

One question the scripture asks is, who can understand his errors, and who can tell how many times we offend.

Who can understand how many times we must have offended God and walked off in a lawless spirit without even knowing it.

The Father is searching for a people who will worship Him in spirit and truth. (John 4:23)

The Word alone – you dry up, the spirit alone – you blow up, the spirit and truth – you grow up.

If there were just a clear dividing line. What may have been obedience for us yesterday may be disobedience for today. God may be trying to bring us into a new sphere of service. As the will of God is revealed, we must walk in that will as it is revealed or we will be guilty of lawlessness.

We can take the truths and gifts of God and walk in disobedience. When we move ahead in our own wisdom and strength to do our own thing, this is sin. We're all familiar with the term, general practitioner in the field of medicine. This same term describes conditions in the church. One person may have been trying to do everything. However, today, God is leading us into specialties. If we don't listen to His directions, should He speak to us in this area, and if we continue to do all of the other things just as before, this becomes disobedience or lawlessness.

What is the antidote for all this? Listen to God! In today's churches, there is a lot of religion and very little obedience. Yesterday and tomorrow are not on God's agenda. It is a today thing! Today, you have the opportunity to obey the Lord.

There is a fine line between obedience and disobedience, faith and presumption, authority and control, anointing and flesh power.

To a believer, who is willing to lay everything at the feet of Jesus, the Holy Spirit will reveal very clearly between these and they will not fall prey to the counterfeit.

One sure way to know something is God is that it flows and it doesn't have to be shoved along, and you don't have to constantly stop and fight the devil off.

With the blessings of God, it's like a big glass tube from one point to another. You see the enemy and all his garbage he tries. You are always a step ahead.

Are you wearing the wrong sign?

Has the enemy been constantly on your path? Are you not functioning up to God's standard? Does your grapevine have lots of healthy leaves but no fruit? Has your peace been replaced with turmoil?

Call out to the Lord. Ask Him to give you the confidence and hunger to search His word for your answers. Begin to pray like never before and spend quiet time in His presence. The more time you spend with Him the quicker you can recognize when things are not right or not according to what God has called you to do.

Seek Him for your gifts and quit trying to do the job He has for others. Get out of the way and let Him operate in your life afresh. You will quickly change your sign and the devil will hate the moment you open your eyes in the morning. Then you can say, " Devil, see my sign now? When He sees you have changed your sign, he will run for the hills.................it works. God's word always works.....Just try it, you will see!

Therefore, as we have opportunity, let us do good to all, especially to those who are of the household of faith. (Galatians 6:10)

Chapter 10

Recognizing Opportunities from God

Many times the Lord visits His people with opportunities which are followed by abundant blessings, but many do not recognize them or they are met with excuses which cancel the blessings.

Do you recognize an opportunity from God or do you look for an excuse because you don't think you can do it or you don't have time or you are just full of fear.

Fear precedes excuses as faith precedes opportunity. Excuses cancel the blessings. They cancel the visitations and miracles of God. We must look for opportunities in every situation. Blessings follow the opportunities of God.

When God brings opportunity our way, He always provides the ability to accomplish what He asks. If you are unwilling to take the opportunity, God will release you from the assignment He brought to you which was an opportunity for great blessing. He will visit someone else. Luke 14: 16-24.

Only by moving in the opportunities God brings our way can we grow and be fulfilled in our lives and ministries.

Only by flowing in God's opportunities, to serve someone else, do you realize the hidden blessings for yourself.

You can never bless someone else without being blessed yourself. You will never be happy or fulfilled until you get into the vein of your anointing. Whatever God asks you to do will directly relate to the anointing upon your life.

God knows where your anointing or gifts lie and His opportunities will be directly in line with them. As you flow in that place, you will grow spiritually and the anointing will increase.

We are at a crossroads in life and ministry. We can remain where we are or go higher with God.

We can choose to be used for His glory or lose His blessings. If we refuse, we lose and if we say "yes" we get blessed. God will always accomplish His purposes whether it's through you or someone else. That's why many Christians never walk in great blessings because they are unwilling to receive God's call to opportunity and instead give every kind of excuse of why certainly they couldn't do that.

God will never override our will. He will ask but He won't force an opportunity upon us. We must make the choice to trust Him enough to know He would never ask us to do something that He wouldn't be there to see us through.

God doesn't want us to fail, he wants successes, but that only comes through yielding totally to Holy Spirit and trusting in His strength and wisdom.

God is grieved many times at our independent spirits. He wants us to depend on Him.

A servant is never independent of his master. He waits for his instructions and then faithfully carries them out. In turn, he is blessed by receiving his needs met.

We have been bought with a price. We have been sealed by the Holy Spirit and have His mark of ownership. Yet, He will never force us to obey. It is a choice, a decision, a heart's desire to yield ourselves totally to His will.

Some have missed great job opportunities because it would have brought change to their lifestyle. Trusting God means change. It means getting out of the familiar, getting out of our place of comfort, getting out of what we are accustomed to. It means launching out into the unfamiliar, moving into areas of discomfort, dealing with unordinary situations. If it is God, He is always there to see you through, giving direction, equipping and giving you peace in every circumstance. The rewards far outweigh the discomforts.

God wants to always challenge us. Challenge brings growth, maturity and it brings a continued reliance on the Spirit of God and not our flesh.

Will you receive and welcome the opportunities of God or will you look for excuses. Will you walk in abundant blessings or complain why God doesn't every send blessings your way? Choose opportunities sent by God and watch the blessings flow!

…to know the love of Christ which passes knowledge; that you may be filled with all the fullness of God. (Ephesians 3:19)

Chapter 11

"No Vacancy"

The Christian should hang a permanent "no vacancy" sign on all areas of his life because he has the Holy Spirit dwelling in him.

When the devil drives by, he knows he's not welcome. There is no use to ever knock at the door.

When there is any uncommitted, un-surrendered area of our life, it's like hanging the "vacancy" sign out and inviting the enemy to come in with dirty feet on God's clean carpet.

We choose what sign we display by an act of our will. Jesus chose to will His life and decisions based on God's will. He only did what the Father said. He reconciled the whole of Himself, mentally and emotionally, by an act of His will to the truth that was revealed to Him.

We are to give the devil no place or opportunity in our lives. It all begins with knowing who you are and whose you are.

The devil wants to keep you blindfolded to who you are in Christ Jesus. He tells us we can't know the things of God and we should trust no one but ourselves.

The truth is that the life-giving spirit has become resident within us. We should stop seeking for things outside and start tuning in on the inside.

Many people don't receive from the Lord for the same reason the world didn't receive Jesus, when He walked the earth.

Jesus Christ was and still is the Living Word, but then He did not conform to their expectations and guidelines. They expected Him to follow their customs and regulations.

Even today when the Lord speaks, most people fail to listen because of their preconceived notions of how God should respond. Then when God gives them an answer, they don't want to hear. They immediately close their mind and heart.

The Lord wants us to be in divine communication with Him, not a second or third party. We can't always depend on another person for direction. Deception can get in when we constantly depend on others for answers.

God uses other vessels, at times, to bring words of direction and instructions. That person should be someone you know that walks with and hears the Lord. Their walk must match their talk. It must, must, must line up with the Word of God, and usually confirm something you have already sensed in your own spirit.

That word should always witness to your spirit, even if it's something you don't want to accept, but deep down you know it's the Lord.

Sometimes, when a word is given, it doesn't come to pass because:
1. God's promises of hope is rejected and the person or persons continue to live in sin. God's word of blessing will not be fulfilled.
2. When people walk in disobedience to the spoken word and refuse to heed the commands of Christ.

The Father has brought us out of the control of the enemy through the blood of Jesus, so the enemy has no power over us, unless we give him control. He deceives to gain power.

The Holy Spirit is to have master control so the whole man is saying, "Yea, yea" to God by mind, will and emotions. Then, a person is no longer fragmented. Jesus came to break down the middle walls of separation.

Some of the Body of Christ is so fragmented that our emotions are in one place, our minds in another, and our wills are somewhere else and there is no agreement.

If you can't control your emotions, you block them off in a corner and your mind won't let you express them. You've created a monster that you're afraid of, so you try to keep your emotions buried.

Jesus was fully in control of His emotions. He could laugh, cry, and show compassion. He wasn't afraid to be tender, but He was totally in touch with His emotions.

To be filled with the Holy Spirit simply means to be controlled by the Holy Spirit.

We need to get deprogramed from the worldly ways. Paul says in Ephesians 4:25, "Rejecting all falsity and done now with it..". Who is supposed to do the rejecting? You.

God puts the spirit of truth in you. He resides within. He said our spirit would bear witness with His spirit, whether a thing is of the Lord or not.

Don't keep the door open by just a crack and say, "Well, maybe that might be partly right". You are leaving out a "vacancy" sign for the enemy....."Room for Compromise".

Paul said in II Corinthians 3:18, "All of us as with unveiled face, beholding, as in a mirror the glory of the Lord, are being transformed into the same image from glory to glory, just as by the Spirit of the Lord".

We are programmed to concentrate on our limitations. There are no limitations in the Lord. Why should we rely on ourselves more than on Him, who is in us in power?

The greater the work God does in you, the greater the work He can do through you.

Fill up to overflowing. Always live and minister out of the overflow and you will never get empty or drained.

Have you been a man pleaser instead of a God pleaser? Are you afraid of offending someone, so you go along with whatever the crowd does and what someone else would have you do?

Have you been deceived to believe you will never get out of debt; your loved ones will never come to the Lord; your body will never be healed?

God's Word is truth and final authority! God's Word says that He wants you to prosper and be in health, even as your soul prospers. (III John:2)

God says, give and it shall be given to you, pressed down, shaken together and running over.....(Luke 6:38).

God says we can claim our whole households – the seed of the righteous shall be delivered. (Proverbs 11:21)

He bore our sicknesses and carried our diseases, by His stripes you are healed. (Isaiah 53:5)

Christ has redeemed us from the curse of the law. (Galatians 3:13)

Is He a respecter of persons or has he stopped doing miracles today. Hebrews 13:8 says that Jesus Christ is the same yesterday, today, and forever.

The devil has kept the body of Christ from receiving the fullness that God has promised long enough.

Do you choose to live in deception or truth, defeat or victory. Do you live by the world or do you live by God's word.

Post your "no vacancy" sign and get into the Word of God. Begin to quote it, pray it and believe it above all other words the world dishes out.

You will walk in a victory and assurance, that will bring peace to you in every circumstance. Just check it out. You have no problem that God hasn't already provided the answer for. Get into His Word...........................you will see!

Phyllis W. Gray

He sends forth springs into the valleys; their waters run among the mountains….(Psalm 104:10)

Chapter 12

Valley Victories – Mountain Top Miracles

A valley speaks of a low place , a deep or difficult place, a place surrounded by higher surfaces. A valley is a place of vulnerability where you're open to be preyed upon by an enemy.

In scripture, valleys are favorite places for battles, places of struggles, places of defeat and despair.

Spiritually speaking, a valley in our lives, speaks of a place where we feel surrounded by circumstances that seem out of control. We have doubts many times about our faith. We despair and sometimes accept defeat.

God never intended for us to give up in the valley. Ezekiel 37 speaks of the valley of dry bones and this is where many churches have been for a long time, a bunch of dry bones. God is sending servants into the dead churches and is breathing the Holy Spirit upon them and they are coming alive!

Psalm 65:9 says, "You visit the earth and saturate it with water; you greatly enrich it; the river of god is full of water".

John 7:38, "He who believes in Me, who cleaves to and trusts in and relies on Me, as the scripture has said, From his innermost being shall flow springs and rivers of living water".

If you're in the valley of despair, doubt, and defeat, God

has provided a river of refreshing. He's provided a way to have victory and come out of the valley.......it's through praise; praising Him in spite of the flesh and feelings.

You will find that river of refreshing through praise! Get into the river of God. There is cleansing, refreshing and the Holy Spirit refueling, power to praise your way out of the valley straight to the mountain tops!

When we praise, we're lifted in the spirit. We are no longer in a low place, but we can look down on our problems and they don't look nearly as big. You are over them. They are no longer over you!

You are able to see with clear eyes and see farther, and the higher you go up, the better your vision is.

Most revelations and miracles take place on the mountain. (Isaiah 56:6-7, 57:13-15, 58:8,11-14)

Mountains speak of high places. Moses was on a mountain when God's glory passed by.

Jesus often went to a mountain to pray. When we are in a valley it's hard to pray.

Jesus was transfigured on a mountain. Satan even showed Jesus the kingdoms of the world from a mountain. In Matthew 15, Jesus ministered from a mountain.

He was crucified upon a hill or mount called Golgatha, and He will come again and set His feet upon the Mount of Olives.

A mountain high place speaks of contact with God.

It is a place of revelation, a place of God's glory, a place of resting before the Lord and a place of total surrender to God.

An eagle builds her nest high in the mountains. When the storms come she doesn't fly down to the valley below, but she soars above the clouds and rides out the storm.

She sees for miles and knows what is ahead. When we are submitted and on the mountain with the Lord through prayer and praise, God gives us clear vision to see ahead. This is where answers will come from, supernatural solutions to problems. This is where your faith will soar and make you strong to stand against any fear or doubt that may come against you.

God didn't make us to be beneath Satan's feet, but he is supposed to be under our feet. God made us to be the head and not the tail. He says that we are more than conquerors. We are overcomers in this life. He is our protector, our provider, our healer, our deliverer, our Savior and soon coming King!

A river flows from the mountain. It's the river of God and it's where the anointing is. It is a place you get so full it flows out of you onto those around you. You will experience His presence and His glory according to the measure of your surrender.

Follow that river of anointing. Come to the mountaintop and allow that river of anointing to flow out of you to others. Allow the Lord to use you, to fill you to overflowing and to use you for what He created you to be.

Call forth your victory in the valley. Praise your way to the river of refreshing. Let it wash off the negative world and it's influences. Rise to the mountain. Then look down at your problems. Let God give you the supernatural answers to situations you're dealing with.

Stay in His presence on the mountain. You don't have to get in the valley anymore. Claim His promises in and for your life.

The world has lied to us. God hasn't changed. He's the same.

Step into the river of God. Drink from the fountain that never runs dry.

Fill up to overflowing on the mountaintop. Receive your miracle and then walk in victory every day, not just sometimes.

Reach out to the Lord and ask Him to fill you to overflowing. Let Him lift you from the valley of despair and defeat to the mountain of miracles and the abundant life God has for you. Remember, it is yours for the asking because He has already paid every price for you.............now, take it!

A man's mind plans his way, but the Lord directs his steps and makes them sure. (Proverbs 16:9 amplified version)

Chapter 13

Where?

Where have you been in life? Where are you now? Where are you headed and most of all where do you belong?

If today you came before God's throne and had to give an account of where you've been in life and what you have done in God's kingdom, what would you say?

Where would you be and what would you be doing today and if asked, what would your plans be for tomorrow?

God had a plan for each of our lives when we were created. Our environment, our family, friends and our own decisions have molded our past and brought us to where we are today.

We have been molded by circumstances and outside pressures of situations in our lives and people we have been surrounded by.

Did you ever have a deep desire to do something as a child, but you were told so many times why you couldn't and you finally believed it and forgot about the inward prompting.

Did you envision dreams of what you'd become in later life and what you'd like to accomplish, but again, circumstances and those you kept company with always steered you in another direction?

Are you happy with where you are today? Have you accomplished the goals and dreams of yesterday? Are you on your way to meeting your dreams and goals of tomorrow? Is what you desire and what God desires the same thing?

Does God have you where you are in life or has man and circumstances influenced you?

Have you been convinced by man or the Holy Spirit about what you can accomplish? Do you have a clear Holy Spirit given picture of where God wants you and what your purpose is? Are you being led by God and influenced by the right kind of people?

You will never grow any higher than the people you associate with. If you want a deeper relationship with God, you have to be with those who have that kind of relationship. We become like that we associate with.

Matthew 6:24 says that no man can serve two masters. You cannot serve God and man!

If a person tries to influence you in a different direction than what God is leading you, draw away, seek the Lord for your answers and ask Him to send people who will encourage you and be of like mind in the things of the Lord.

Do you hear the Lord in decisions you make or do you make them because you think it will please someone else? You will be accepted by the crowd, who seems to be blessed while doing these things.

Do you have a perfect peace in your heart or are you at ill-ease about where you are in life?

You can't change your past and you can't change what you were when you awoke this morning, but you can change where you'll be and what you'll be doing tomorrow and the days thereafter!

We have become a people pleasing society. That is why our streets are full of kids on drugs. It is the "in" thing, that makes them accepted by their peers who are doing it.

If you have ever drank or taken drugs because you were following the crowd, you knew you were doing it for the wrong reasons, but through encouragement from peers who provided that pressure, you did it anyway.

God is looking for a "strong" man or woman that will say, "I will follow Jesus no matter what others do"!

This is not always easy, because many Christians spend more time socializing with friends than they spend with the Lord. No wonder we follow man instead of God!

God knows our hearts. He knows if we are willing to be led by Him or if we will follow after man, or man's desires.

Are you where God wants you today? Are you doing today what He created you for? If not, what do you need to change in your life? Are you at peace in your spirit about where you are in your walk with the Lord?

You must let yesterday die to live today where He's called you to walk and to move into the peace and victories He has for you tomorrow.

Are you willing to let the past die so your future can be alive? If you are living in hurts of the past, you will continue to take them into your future unless you get rid of them today.

All ties of the past and present must be broken and allowed to die in order to move into the future free, at peace, and available for the Lord to use you for what He has called you to do.

God knew you before you were formed. He knew things you would encounter along life's way, but He equipped you with that heart that would seek Him and He put all the tools there to be used for your victory and His glory.

He filled you with His spirit to accomplish everything He

created you for.

It is up to you to allow the Holy Spirit to be your guiding influence, not your past, not your friends, not your circumstances or situations, not any outside interference, only the Holy Spirit's leading.

He wants a "strong" man or woman that will stand on His Word, at all costs to see His glory and His will bring change in their life.

Have outside influences held you back from becoming all you could be? It is never too late, in God's eyes to allow Him to take control of your life.

You just need to release the controls to Him and let Him pilot your life. Spend time in His Word. Learn the scriptures so when adversity or diversions come, you can speak the Word against it and be able to stand without wavering.

Become strong by feeding on His Word. Become strong by spending time with the Master. You can be used for His glory no matter what your past ties are.

Begin today to turn the other way and leave the past behind. Let go of the dead things that drag you down and start fresh. Look to the future with dreams again and pray, believe and begin to act on those dreams. Only listen to God's Word that says who you are and positive people that will build you up and not drag you down. You are on a mission now to fulfill what God has for you.

Get to it! Don't quit! Know that He is with you every step of the way! Your future holds blessings and fulfilled dreams that you cannot even imagine. Now.....take His hand and make it happen!

The preparations of the heart belong to man, but the answer of the tongue is from the Lord. All the ways of man are pure in his own eyes, but the Lord weighs the spirits. Commit your works to the Lord and your thoughts will be established. (Proverbs 16: 1-3)

Chapter 14

Our Choices Determine Our Lives

Where we are today has been determined by the choices we have made in the past. We, so often, blame others when things haven't turned out the way we thought they would. Our todays are products of the choices we made in our past and will determine where we are in days ahead unless we reverse some choices. Our destinies are determined by our choices, not by chance.

You make choices daily, whether you realize it or not, sometimes many choices. We take these things for granted and only look at how things turn out when we expect good and end up with a mess.

If we look back at our past, we can see how we have made wrong decisions that determined our todays.

How do we know to make right decisions or choices in life? The first thing we must do is pray and wait until we hear from God. He has every answer we need and knows every choice we should make. We get busy and in a hurry, so we make decisions quickly without waiting on the Lord.

Without His direction in our lives, we inevitably will make choices that will bring more problems and not the results we expected.

Spending part of our day with the Lord will help set our thinking straight and our choices will be based on God's direction and His word in our lives, rather than what seems right or what someone else has told us is right. We cannot follow man and make good choices. We can be easily led astray and get into deception and compromise when we listen to people rather than searching for our answers from the Lord. Our heart is already telling us that it's the wrong choice. We don't listen and continue to go down that path, knowing it isn't right. Finally we end up at a crossroad where we must continue on that path or turn and take another direction.

This is when we must seek the Lord, ask His forgiveness for not listening to His spirit. Following our flesh has led us the wrong way, now, we must wait on the Lord for new direction.

These choices will determine where we will walk in our future. Will they have the blessings of God on them or will we end up in a mess again?

Determine today to seek Him always before making any choice. He will never lead you wrong nor speak deception to you.

If you base your choices on His word and His voice as you spend time in His presence, He will order your steps, direct your path, and keep you from stumbling.

Your choices will give you blessed days ahead. The days will give you hope, joy, peace and blessings you never imagined.

Seek Jesus. He will always give you the right direction for your life. Every tomorrow will be full of joy and His glory.

Choose His way, He will never lead you astray.

Begin today, you will be glad you did!

Let the word of Christ dwell in you richly in all wisdom, teaching and admonishing one another in psalms and hymns and spiritual songs, singing with grace in your hearts to the Lord. (Colossians 4:16)

Chapter 15

Are You Filled With God's Word or Man's World?

Everywhere we look today there is news about things we cannot control, yet these things often control how we live. We hear the weather and decide it will determine what kind of day we will have by what the report says, rain or sun.

The news media gives an update on the stock market and if it's down and we have investments we panic or if up, then we are encouraged.

Oh, and when we hear that gas prices are going to soar or the price of milk and food staples are rising again then our mind begins to make us reason how we will fit that into our already tight budget. We have already determined that we probably won't ever get another raise at our job, and we might not even have that for long if things keep up the way they are.

Gloom and doom is what we hear from the world on a daily basis. We really have to listen to a lot of negative to find a few positive things. No wonder over half of our population is walking around with no joy, no peace and no hope for a better future.

Jobs today are hard to come by. So many people are unemployed or underemployed because of the economy. This is all true, BUT..............if the word of God is bigger in us that the words of the world, we will not be influenced by what the world says. We will take God's word and His promises and believe that His word works and will guide our lives in the days ahead instead of what the six o'clock news said. It's hard! Oh, yes it's hard not to listen and live by what you hear every day, but what you feed your spirit on a daily basis is what it will produce. Garbage in and garbage out or God's word in and His promises come out of our mouth instead of negative words and actions.

So many people who call themselves Christians are word starved. They love the Lord and are faithful to what they know, but what they don't know is destroying them. They have never been taught that there are promises in God's word that are truth and work today the same as they did over 2000 years ago. They feel that one day, when they get to Heaven, things will be different.

Some churches over the years, discouraged people from reading the word, for fear they might misinterpret it, and others preach hellfire and damnation, and then we have the social church that only makes the people feel good when they come and socialize.

Praise God, the church is coming alive again! Almost every denomination is now encouraging Bible reading and studies among the congregation. There are numerous seminars and retreats being given to draw people closer to God through His word. The spirit of God is at work to draw His body together, to educate them and send them out to gather in the harvest. How can we be a blessing to others if we are not blessed? Who wants to listen to someone who is a failure at what he is doing or lives on barely get by street? People are looking for role models in this world.

If our lives are patterned after God's word and it is working for us, then others will want to know how we are prospering in a dying economy and why we always have a smile on our face and a pep in our step. We are being watched by others every day and we are a good witness or a poor one by the way we are living. Instead of going to work every day dreading what may lie ahead, we can go believing that we can do all things through Christ who strengthens us which is taken from Philippians 4:13. We can work as unto the Lord in all we do and believe that what we do will prosper according to Psalm 1:3.

God's word is full of these promises. They apply to every walk of life, no matter what we are going through. We just have to know they are there and begin to read them, believe them and act on them.

If someone gave us a gift and we never opened it, then we would never know what it contained and would not profit from it. It is the same way with God's word. He has given us everything we will ever need to live a victorious life, but if we don't read the Promise Book, then we will never know what He has promised us.

I have to say here, that without the promises of God and knowing what His word says pertaining to my life, I would have been dead long ago. I have walked through many valleys and suffered a great deal of heartache in my life, but because I wouldn't give up and kept the word of God in my mouth day and night, God delivered me from every pitfall and today I am so blessed.

I wish I could open up every reader and pour the word of God inside. It only comes from hearing, hearing, and hearing. As we read His word, even then we are hearing with our spirit. When we watch a minister delivering a message, we are hearing the word of God. When we sing worship songs, we are hearing the word of God. It's not boring to read the word. It is exciting! If we will begin to write down some of the scriptures that have meaning to us for a trial we are going through, then as we read it again and again, the words will become real and we will find we are believing them above what the world says.

This is what we must do. Put God's word first above all else the world says. If the world says that things are getting

worse and worse, we have to begin to confess what
God's word says about the situation. Believe what the word
says rather than what the world says. Yes, people may think
you a little weird, but when you are prospering, paying your
bills and getting a promotion, then they will see whose way is
working.

God's word works! It always does. It may not be just like we
think the answer will come but the answer will come! God
nor His word ever fails. We fail because we so many times
waiver in what we believe. Standing on the word is
mandatory until you see the answer. It's like praying the
pure word of God over a situation, it will always produce
results if we believe.

Do you know the word of God? Do you put it to work in your
daily life? Do you read it and study it, listen to it, sing it?
If not, it's never too late to begin. As in an earlier chapter,
what you do today determines what your tomorrow will be
like.

Get with people who live the word of God. Watch and
observe their lives, then begin to ask the Lord to help you
glean truths from His word as you read it. Put to memory
some of the meaningful scriptures that stand out to you.
Write a few at a time on a note and carry them with you. Pull
them out several times a day and read them. It won't take
long and you will be quoting them from memory. Also you
will find your spirit will bring them up when you need them
most.

We can't depend on a church or person to teach us what we
need to know. It is up to us to get what we need for our daily
life. We can live in daily defeat or we can live in daily victory.
We can be joyful, at peace and trusting in the Lord in all we
do or we can be depressed, angry and resentful toward every
person, blaming others for our problems.

Again, it's choices we make. God's word or the world's

words, which do you choose to live by? Only we can decide from this day forth how we will live the rest of our life. We cannot blame others for our poor judgment.

God has made the provisions. It is up to us to decide to make use of them and set our life in a different direction. Only God's word can change our life for the better. Nothing this world has to offer can ever make us happy or bring us a better life.

We are His workmanship. He is the Master Carpenter and He has fashioned us after Himself. He has provided the Handbook(Bible) for us to follow. It contains all we will ever need to live a good, victorious life.

Pick up the book. Read it. Study it. Put the words into practice and watch what happens in your life!

*Trust in the Lord with all your heart.
Lean not to your own understanding,
but in all your ways acknowledge
Him and He will direct your path.
(Proverbs 3:5-6)*

Chapter 16

A Step Back is Not a Setback

In our daily lives, we must periodically examine our path to see if we are following the plan God has set before us.

When things aren't going the way we think they should, or not as quick as we wanted them, then discouragement sets in and we call it a setback.

We need not accept setbacks when all we need to do is step back and do an assessment of our situation and make a few changes in the plan.

This is why daily prayer is so important. By talking with the Lord every day, we will always be in the know when it comes to bumps in the road or obstacles in our path that we must avoid. We will not be caught off guard or be surprised by things that would cause us problems ahead.

The Lord will prepare us daily for our journey and make us aware when the path is treacherous.

When we trust Him for our lives, He directs our paths. Proverbs 3:5-6, "Trust in the Lord with all your heart. Lean not to your own understanding. In all your ways, acknowledge Him and He will direct your path". That is one of my favorite scriptures, because if we follow it in life, we will not fail.

God never creates or causes setbacks for us. There are times He may ask us to step back and look. When we do this we see where we have come from and see where we are headed.

If we don't know what we have come through, we can't appreciate the grace and favor God gives us daily.

Every day we should pray Gods' blessings, favor and grace over us and our family. During the day we should continue to thank Him for it and watch it work over and over.

When things hinder the plan, step back, thank God for His help and look at the situation through the eyes of your spirit, not in the natural.

Let God's word rise in your heart and don't be moved at what things look like but remember what the scripture says and hold to that. Don't waiver!

Step back. Regain your confidence through His word and never declare a setback.

When you declare a setback you give the enemy ground to discourage you into believing you have failed. Sometimes, it is hard to move ahead when you feel you are back to where you started.

With a step back, you declare to the enemy that you are not giving him any authority. You, with God's help, are in control and are only planning your next steps.

Life is all about the choices we make that determines our path toward what kind of life we have.

Failures are caused by accepting one setback after another and never moving forward in the right direction.

Accepting defeat to some is the easy way out. They continually make excuses for why they never get ahead. Bad luck is the reason they use or they were not treated fairly.

Excuses are the quitter's way out. Those who make them wallow in their defeat, then make more excuses by playing the blame game. It's everyone else's fault, but definitely not theirs.

Moving ahead will always have obstacles, but its success instead of failure. You never fail until you quit. Our obstacles become step backs instead of setbacks.

Show up every morning for your orders for the day from your Commander –in-Chief. He always knows what is ahead and will prepare you for your day. He's the "Master Planner" and will never lead you astray.

Move ahead with dreams and plans, accepting God's direction along the way. You may have a time in your day when you need to step back for adjustments in the plan, but you will never accept a setback again.

"I called on the Lord in distress; The Lord answered me and set me in a broad place. The Lord is on my side; I will not fear. What can man do to me? The Lord is for me among those who help me;" (Psalm 118:5-7)

Chapter 17

Insolation vs Isolation

Our human nature tends to separate us from others when adversity comes our way. We don't want to bother others with our troubles and we feel sure we can deal with it better if we don't involve anyone else.

Our mind plays over the words of "nobody is interested in your problems", or "so you are alone, don't go be a third shoe". No matter what the issue we are facing, negativity will always try to creep in and make us feel like we are the only one on the earth facing such a crisis. This is one of the greatest ploys of the enemy to get us to isolate ourselves from the very ones that could bring us up out of the pit we are in.

This is especially true when a tragedy happens. It doesn't matter whether it is the death of a loved one or even the loss of a job, it is still a traumatic situation.

At first you are usually surrounded by friends and other family, and those who are supporting you through whatever the situation is. But the days come later when no one else is around and you have to begin to deal with what has happened and that is when your mind works overtime to try to discourage you.

This is where the big mistake is made to isolate yourself from anything and anyone in order to finally come to grips with what has happened. THAT is not the way to deal with anything! When we isolate from others and things we are very vulnerable to deception if we are not walking very closely with the Lord. Even then it is very difficult to keep focused on the positive and allow healing and a new perspective on things if we separate ourselves from those who love and care for us.

We as friends tend to believe sometimes that when we know someone who is going through this kind of situation, that perhaps they want to be left alone and we back off and don't call or visit even though we are thinking of them. This is when we need to go out of our way to send them a card, give them a phone call or just drop by and perhaps take them to lunch.

It will be at the very time they needed someone to talk to or get a hug from or receive a word of encouragement or just see a person that really cares and understands what they are going through.

Isolation is destructive! It can be deadly! This is the time when so many people commit suicide. They listen to the voices that tell them they can't possibly go on and get over the situation. They feel that no one cares anymore and they finally give in and take their life.

Isolation is like being in a cave with no light or air to breathe. It makes you feel like there is no way out. At first you wanted to be here to hide in hopes that all this would just go away and things would be the way they were before, but the longer you stay in isolation the more the life is being sucked out of you and you get the feeling that you just don't care anymore because no one else does so why should you.

God never isolates us from love and affection! He may separate us from familiar things at times to get our attention, especially if He has an assignment for us to take care of that requires more focus on Him and His Word to accomplish.

He will fulfill our needs with other friends and places so we will not be totally isolated from the things we love.

He will insolate us with His love and His Word and lead us to reach out to others in our time of despair. It is in times of need that we draw strength from helping others and reaching out to those who also have needs.

When we insolate our lives with people who have needs, it will draw from our inner being, strength we did not know we had and if we have planted God's Word within our hearts, that word will come up and out to help those we reach out to. Not only those but it will help us too!

When we allow the love of God and our friends and family to surround us, it is like putting on a warm coat in cold weather. It feels warm and cozy and we are not shivering anymore because the warmth insolates us from the cold.

Love insolates us from despair, depression, aloneness, and hopelessness. It will fill our heart and life with purpose, encouragement, and a reason to be needed by others. We will see things through entirely different eyes than what we were seeing before. It will make us realize that our problem is not as big as those we see around us and God, many times, will let us meet someone who is going through the same thing we are dealing with.

We can't stay in our cave of isolation, but we must come out and begin to insolate ourselves with those around us who love us and want to help us. We in turn, can reach out to others and we will begin to heal and things in our lives will become better, our outlook will be more positive and then we can truly see God's hand in it all.

He loves us and He wants us to lean on and depend on Him to direct us in our good times and our bad times.

He has all the answers and longs for us to be happy, healthy, prosperous and a blessing to others. As we are a blessing, we are blessed and in our tragedies we heal, grow and help others to heal also. We can turn tragedies into triumphs in our lives by refusing isolation and reaching and encompassing insolation. It will make the difference in our future and the future of all those we touch in the process.

I know this to be true, because I went through this very thing. I write this because this is exactly what the Lord spoke to me one morning when I was so far down in the cave of despair.

It wasn't easy to come out because I had made a place to lay and wallow in my misery. When I heard His voice and the words He spoke, I knew I had to get up and fight my way out of the darkness to the light of His love.

I did and I began to reach out to others and make my friends a part of my life again. It was such healing to help others and then, there was my writing. That is how the first book, "Quiet Moments In His Presence" came about. It was the Lord speaking to me, loving me with His Word and allowing me to write and bring healing to me, and now I pray to all who read it. It is through writing that I have been able to express my heart, and God's teachings that He has given me over the last years.

Remember Isolation brings death! Insolation through love brings new life not only to you but to all the others whose lives you touch.

"Fear not, for I have redeemed you; I have called you by your name; You are mine. When you pass through the waters, I will be with you; And through the rivers, they shall not overflow you. When you walk through the fire, you shall not be burned, nor shall the flame scorch you, for I am the Lord your God. (Isaiah 43:1-3)

Chapter 18

Not THE END, It's THE BEGINNING

I cannot justly write, "THE END" to this book, because as you are finishing this, it is the first day of the rest of your life! Every time you read from these writings you are able to declare a new day in your life. Every sunrise and every sunset signals the beginning and ending of our day, but each one is a new beginning!

We have the ability to change our destiny every single day when the sun rises and make decisions that will bring change before the sun sets.

I pray you are inspired to spend time every day with the Lord and allow Him to direct your life in the way He wants you to go. Learn to listen in the quiet moments of your day, wherever they are, even if only a few moments at a time. Believe me, God doesn't need all day to get a message across to you if you are willing and eager to hear from Him. He knows us, individually and He is aware of the time we actually have in our daily lives.

He is with us every moment of every day and He doesn't leave just because we get busy. He patiently waits on us, ready to listen when we call out to Him. When God gave the title of this book to me, I realized the significance of it. I talk to the Lord morning, noon and night or just whenever I want to talk to Him. During most days, I am alone when my husband is at work and I just know the Lord is right here and if I want to say something or pray about a concern, I just talk and talk. It has made Him so real to me that I never doubt that He goes with me wherever I go and is always ready to listen to what I have to say. He really cares that much for each of us and loves us enough to always be ready to listen when we talk to Him.

I, for years, said I was going to write a book, more than one time and then procrastinated about it. My first book, "Quiet Moments In His Presence" came about from notes that I was writing at night when I couldn't sleep and the Lord would talk to me and I would write it down. Little did I know that these writings would become a book.

This book, has been different because as the Lord gave me some of these writings I knew they would be a part of my next book. These chapters and this book will not become a best seller or be in every household, but if only one heart is changed, touched and given a new hope in life, then I have achieved what I begun. My only desire as I record what the Lord gives me is to share His direction and love in the words that come forth.

My life has been forever changed since I have started putting on paper what I hear the Spirit of God say. I know these words are not for just me but the body of Christ and that is why I put them on paper. I feel so rich when I read what I have written and know I am not the author but the penman and all the glory goes to my Lord and Savior, Jesus Christ.

If you don't know Jesus as your Savior, or you aren't sure, just simply ask Him to come into your heart and forgive you of all your sins and shortcomings. He will welcome you with open arms and wipe the slate of your life clean and give you a new beginning. It will be the most wonderful thing you have ever done.

If you do know Him as your Lord and Savior, then don't forget to take the time daily to tell Him how much you love Him and thank Him for all His blessings in your life. Being grateful opens the door to many more blessings. We can't ever praise Him too much, after all, He gave everything, His life, for us. Can we give Him some time every day, thanking and praising and just having a talk with Him? You can't even imagine how wonderful it will make you feel and what it will do in your everyday life. Things around us can be frantic and all in disarray, but when we know who we are and whose we are, we can still carry the peace of God in our hearts.

Cast all that care on Him. He cares for you. As the scripture at the beginning of this chapter says, "Fear not". He is with you and He will always be if you let Him be your Lord, Savior, Healer, Deliverer, and soon coming King. He will be all of them if you will reach out to Him and allow Him into your life.

Many prayers to everyone reading this book. Share it with others and I pray it makes a difference in every life it touches. God's richest blessings to you and may you be filled with all the fullness of God's love and grace.

About The Author

Phyllis was born and lived most of her life in central North Carolina. She is married to Ike Gray and they now reside in Hawaii.

She has a Doctorate degree in Christian Education from Jacksonville Theological Seminary and has been an ordained minister for over 25 years. She has traveled as an evangelist in the U.S. and abroad sharing God's Word. She had a daily radio program for 5 years and today maintains a ministry website, Voices of Victory/Phyllis Gray Ministries. She enjoyed writing at an early age, but only seriously in the last few years.

Phyllis has lived what she writes and has relied on God's Word to take her through many tough places in her life. Her writings show how God has ministered to her and gave her what she needed to become an overcomer. She has a heart for those seeking a deeper walk with the Lord.

She and her husband love sharing and ministering to the homeless where they live in Hawaii. She believes every day is a blessing and God wants us to share those blessings with others.

Phyllis W. Gray

Visit our website for more ministry articles and newsletters.
www.voicesofvictory.com

Watch for the next book coming out by early 2015..................

Title: "It Had To Be God"   the story of Phyllis's life and how God has
led her many times from tragedy to triumph. Also, be blessed as she
shares the miracles she has witnessed in her life and the lives of others.

All proceeds from sales of this book will go to providing copies to the homeless and those less fortunate. God bless you and thank you for letting us share God's Word and blessings with you.

Ike and Phyllis Gray

Cover photo: Taken by Ike Gray at Sunset Beach, North Shore, Oahu
Other photos: taken by Phyllis Gray

Made in the USA
Columbia, SC
16 October 2023

24151603R00072